W9-AZC-879

STECK-VAUGHN
PORTRAIT OF AMERICA

California

973
POR

California

c1

Albany, NY 12208

Albany, NY 12208

Copyright © 1996 Steck-Vaughn Company

All rights reserved. No part of this book may be reproduced or utilized in any form or by any means, electronic or mechanical, including photocopying, recording, or by any information storage and retrieval system, without permission in writing from the copyright owner. Requests for permission to make copies of any part of the work should be mailed to: Copyright Permissions, Steck-Vaughn Company, P.O. Box 26015, Austin, Texas 78755.

Steck-Vaughn Company
Executive Editor	Diane Sharpe
Senior Editor	Martin S. Saiewitz
Design Manager	Pamela Heaney
Photo Editor	Margie Foster

Proof Positive/Farrowlyne Associates, Inc.
Program Editorial, Revision Development, Design, and Production

Consultant: William T. George, Jr., Assistant Secretary, California Trade and Commerce Agency

Published by Raintree Steck-Vaughn Publishers, an imprint of Steck-Vaughn Company.

A Turner Educational Services, Inc. book. Based on the Portrait of America television series by R. E. (Ted) Turner.

Library of Congress Cataloging-in-Publication Data

Thompson, Kathleen.
  California / Kathleen Thompson.
    p.   cm. — (Portrait of America)
  "Based on the Portrait of America television series"—T.p. verso.
  "A Turner book."
  Includes index.
  ISBN 0-8114-7325-2 (library binding).—ISBN 0-8114-7430-5 (softcover)
  1. California—Juvenile literature. I. Title. II. Series:
Thompson, Kathleen. Portrait of America.
F861.3.T48 1996
979.4—dc20
                                                    95-9610
                                                      CIP
                                                      AC

Printed and Bound in the United States of America

3 4 5 6 7 8 9 10 WZ 03 02 01 00 99

Acknowledgments
The publishers wish to thank the following for permission to reproduce photographs:
P. 7 © Comstock; p. 8 Seaver Center for Western History Research, Natural History Museum of Los Angeles County; p. 10 San Diego Convention and Visitors Bureau; p. 11 North Wind Picture Archives; p. 12 Seaver Center for Western History Research, Natural History Museum of Los Angeles County; p. 13 (both) California State Library; pp. 14–17 Seaver Center for Western History Research, Natural History Museum of Los Angeles County; p. 19 (both) National Portrait Gallery, Smithsonian Institution; p. 20 San Francisco Convention and Visitors Bureau; p. 21 (left) United States Geological Survey, (right) Reuters/Bettmann; pp. 22, 24 © Comstock; p. 25 (top) California Division of Tourism, (bottom) Douglas Aircraft Company; p. 26 (top) National Park Service, (bottom) San Francisco Convention and Visitor's Bureau; p. 27 (top) Michael Reagan, (bottom) California Division of Tourism; p. 28 San Jose Convention and Visitor's Bureau; p. 29 Advanced Micro Devices; p. 30 © Reza Estakhrian/Tony Stone; p. 32 (both) San Francisco Convention and Visitor's Bureau; p. 33 (top) Bancroft Library, (bottom) California Division of Tourism; p. 34 (top) San Diego Zoological Society, (bottom) © David Young-Wolf/PhotoEdit; p. 35 (top) Fresno Chamber of Commerce, (bottom) © Tony Freeman/PhotoEdit; pp. 36, 37 University of Southern California; pp. 38, 39 Movie Stills Archive; pp. 40-41 (both) © Paramount/Shooting Star; p. 42 © The Stock Market; p. 44 Courtesy Apple Computer; p. 46 One Mile Up; p. 47 (top left) Academy of Natural Sciences, (top right) California Office of Tourism, (bottom) One Mile Up.

STECK-VAUGHN

PORTRAIT OF AMERICA

California

Kathleen Thompson

A Turner Book

RSVP

RAINTREE
STECK-VAUGHN
PUBLISHERS
The Steck-Vaughn Company

Austin, Texas

California

Eureka

Sacramento River

Fort Ross

SACRAMENTO

Sonoma

San Francisco • Oakland

San Jose

YOSEMITE
NATIONAL
PARK

SIERRA NEVADA

San Joaquin River

Monterey

• Fresno

SEQUOIA
NATIONAL
PARK

DEATH
VALLEY

Mt. Whitney

Santa Barbara

• Los Angeles

• Anaheim

Colorado River

Long Beach

• San Diego

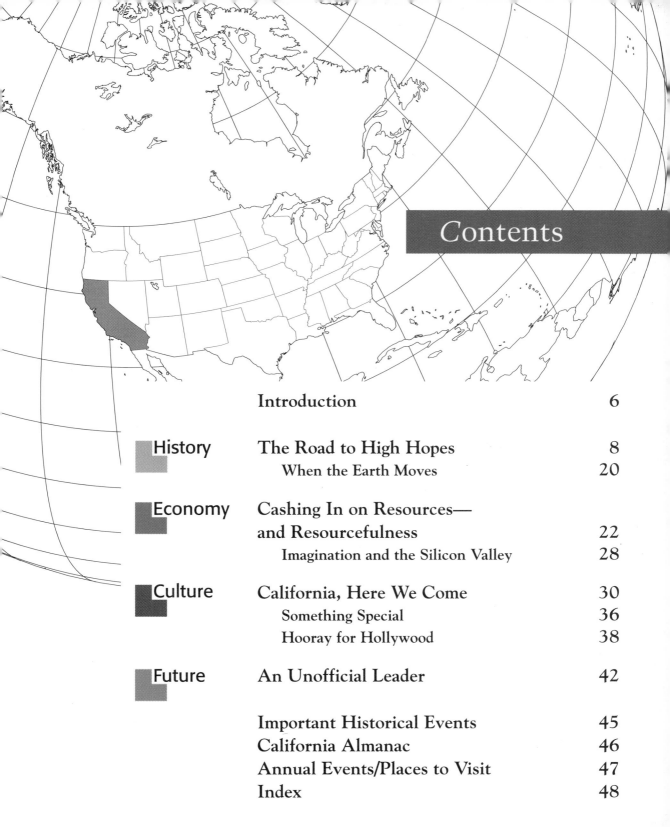

Contents

Introduction

Of all the states, California is usually first with the most. More people call it home than any other state. It has the most good farmland. It overflows with timber and minerals. And Californians excel in combining dreams and hard work to make the most of these rich resources. Today, their state leads the nation in agriculture and manufacturing. The state plays a starring role in the entertainment industry.

Even California's disasters are larger than life. Pollution, earthquakes, floods, and fires have sometimes threatened to turn people's dreams into nightmares. But time after time, Californians dust off their dreams and work to make them come true.

California is a state of great scenic beauty, and it is rich in natural resources.

California

computers, missions, grapes, casual living

The Road to High Hopes

In the years before European settlers came to California, thousands of Native Americans lived in this vast and beautiful region. They lived in villages of one hundred to five hundred people. Most of their food was taken from the ocean, lakes, and rivers. They collected vegetables and seeds that grew in the wild. Very little farming could be found in California. Through the 1600s the Native Americans lived in peace.

In 1540 a Spanish explorer named Hernando de Alarcón sailed up the lower Colorado River. The group he was with saw California but did not explore it. The first European expedition to explore any part of the region was led by Juan Rodríguez Cabrillo. They probably explored the entire coastline up to Oregon. These explorers were looking for two things: gold and a way to go from the Atlantic Ocean to the Pacific Ocean by boat. Their efforts were unsuccessful.

In the early 1600s, Sebastián Vizcaíno explored the coast carefully and reported back to Spain that

Miners found gold in the form of dust, flakes, and nuggets in streambeds. These prospectors use a sluice to control the water flow from a nearby source.

Built in 1769, Mission San Diego de Alcala is the oldest of California's mission churches.

California should be colonized. Spanish leaders in America agreed because they feared that other European powers would want California. In 1579 Francis Drake had claimed California for the British. But no Spanish arrived in California for almost another hundred years.

Then, in 1697, Catholic missionaries came into Lower California, the Mexican peninsula south of what is now the state of California. These people were sent by Spain to convert the people of California to Christianity. The missionaries believed that the Native Americans should give up the religion and the way of life that had been theirs for thousands of years. The Native Americans did not want to change, however. Many were killed when they resisted the new religion. Later the missionaries moved north into Upper California, what is now the state of California.

In the meantime, Russia was showing signs of interest in Upper California. Spain began to get worried. The Spanish government set up outposts at San Diego and Monterey. California was now considered a part of New Spain—at least by the Spaniards.

From 1769 to 1823, Franciscan missionaries built missions along the Pacific Coast. Father Junípero Serra established the first misson at present-day San Diego. The missions were not just churches. The missionaries raised cattle, irrigated the land, and traded hides and tallow to foreign countries. Father Serra established 8 missions, including those at Monterey, San Francisco, and Santa Barbara. The Native Americans were used very much like slaves at the missions. Many of them died of illness and overwork.

In 1810 Mexicans began to fight for freedom from Spanish rule. Mexico became independent in 1821. Spain gave up its claim to California a year later and the area became part of Mexico. All of California was now a part of the newly freed Mexico. The people of California traded freely with other countries. The Russians traded with Californians at the post called Fort Ross that the Russians set up in 1812. In 1826 traders and trappers from the United States traveled overland to California. The first was a man named Jedediah Strong Smith. Many others followed, including Kit Carson.

Between 1833 and 1840, Spanish-Mexican settlers known as *Californios* closed missions and sold their land to ranchers. Some of these ranches ranged up to nearly fifty thousand acres in size.

After about 1840, immigrants from the United States came to California. California accepted citizens from the United States graciously, but more and more, these newcomers wanted to break away from Mexico. Some wanted California to become an independent republic. Some wanted it to become part of the United States. President Andrew Jackson offered to buy the northern part of California. His offer was turned down.

Then Captain John C. Frémont came to California. Captain Frémont's job was surveying

In 1843–1844 John Frémont explored the least-known parts of the West: from the Colorado Rockies to California's Sierra Nevada range.

John Sutter tried to keep the news of a gold strike on his land a secret, but the news leaked out.

for the United States government. However, his actions looked suspicious to the California Mexicans. On June 14, 1846, Frémont broke the peace. He encouraged a group of settlers to take over the province's northern headquarters at Sonoma.

This rebellious group of pioneers and frontiersmen promptly lowered the Mexican flag and raised another over the fort. And it was not the flag of the United States that they hoisted into the air. It was a homemade banner. The rebels were ready to declare California's independence. What this little group didn't know was that Mexico and the United States had gone to war one month before. The two countries were fighting primarily about Texas, not California. But the result of the war would be that both would become part of the United States of America. In 1848 Mexico and the United States signed the Treaty of Guadalupe Hidalgo, making California a part of the United States.

In that same year, a carpenter named James W. Marshall was building a mill on the American River for John Sutter. While building Sutter's Mill, he discovered gold—nuggets of gold. News of the discovery spread rapidly. Suddenly, California was flooded with people looking for gold. They came by the thousands, hungry for sudden wealth. About eighty thousand people came to California in 1849 alone. Some walked; others rode horses alone or in small groups. Many others came by ship around the southern tip of South America. Still others joined caravans of wagons, inching slowly across the two thousand miles between the Missouri River and the Pacific Coast.

The miners made a lot of money and they spent it as fast as they made it. During this time, gold turned San Francisco into a glittering city. Gold built the theaters, banks, and hotels. The men who didn't find gold started farms or went into business in town. The growing population created a need for doctors, tailors, and grocers, to name a few. In 1850 California became the thirty-first state. By 1860 the state's population was almost four hundred thousand.

above. James W. Marshall.

below. This photograph shows James W. Marshall as a young man, standing in front of Sutter's Mill.

Thousands of Chinese laborers helped build the Central Pacific Railroad. This photograph was taken during the construction of a trestle over Secrettown Ravine, about 64 miles east of Sacramento.

When the Civil War ended, there was another rush of people into the state. This time, instead of gold, they were looking for cheap land and high wages. Many Chinese men moved to California to work on the building of the new Central Pacific Railroad. They sent the money they earned back to China to pay for their families to move to America.

By 1870 the mining was slowing down and the railroad was built. Jobs became scarce. Then the Central Pacific fired thousands of Chinese workers who were no longer needed to lay the tracks. When those Chinese workers flooded San Francisco looking for work, riots broke out. There were also riots in Los Angeles. Many workers blamed their unemployment on the Chinese. In 1882 the United States passed a law forbidding Chinese immigrants to enter the country. The Chinese people who were already in California were discriminated against and abused.

California continued to grow. In the 1880s there was a real estate boom and another rush of people came into the state. Disaster hit in 1906 when San Francisco was almost completely destroyed by a huge earthquake and the fires that followed. But the people of San Francisco began to rebuild their city.

About that time, relations between the United States and Japan became strained as Japan gained power in Asia. In 1906 the San Francisco school board ordered the segregation of Japanese, Chinese, and

The photograph shows some of the devastation caused by the San Francisco earthquake of 1906. The Valencia Hotel sank six feet into the earth when an underground streambed collapsed beneath it.

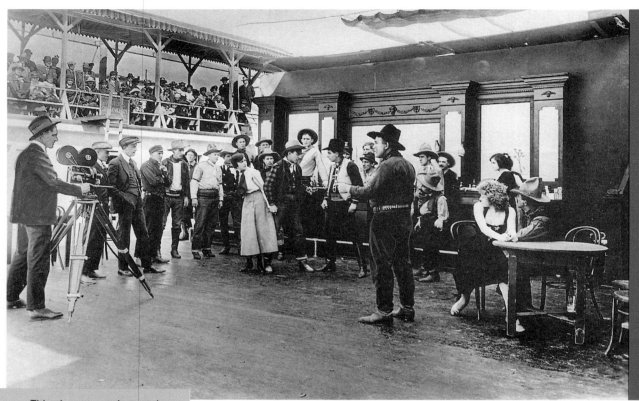

This photo was taken on the set of a silent era Hollywood Western. Galleries above the stage allowed spectators to observe the actors and the crew during filming.

Korean children into separate schools. In 1907 the United States and Japan made a "Gentleman's Agreement" that no more Japanese people would immigrate into the United States. This policy lasted for many years. In 1913 the California legislature considered a law preventing Japanese people from owning land in California.

By this time, gold mining was no longer the basis of California's economy. Because of irrigation, farming was becoming more important. Manufacturing began to grow after oil fields were opened. And, of course, the movie industry became big business in southern

California. By the 1920s Hollywood was the movie capital of the world.

The Great Depression fell upon the country in the 1930s. California was not hit as hard as most of the country at first. But then another wave of immigrants settled into the state. These people came from the "Dust Bowl" states of Colorado, Kansas, Texas, Oklahoma, and New Mexico. A terrible drought in this region wiped out the farmland. The people had lost their farms and stores. The banks had taken away their homes. They had nothing but what they could carry with them. They came to California looking for work. They would work for very low wages. As a result, many higher-paid Californians lost their jobs. Soon California passed a variety of laws to deal with the poor.

Discrimination against Asians came up again after the Japanese attack on Pearl Harbor in 1941. The United States government forced over 100,000 Japanese American citizens into internment camps. There they remained until the end of the war. More than two-thirds of those detained were *nisei*, native-born Americans whose only crime was their ancestry. The nisei lost most of their belongings as they were forced to sell their homes, businesses, and farms at low prices.

A worker completes the assembly of a P-38 fighter plane. During World War II, California factories produced aircraft for the war effort.

When the United States entered World War II, California became a center of aircraft manufacturing. The economy of the state prospered. Many poor Mexican Americans left the rural areas for jobs in the cities. Despite low wages, their lives were improved.

After World War II, many people who had been stationed in California in the armed forces decided to stay. The economy boomed. With more factories and cars came more pollution—in the water and in the air. The word *smog* was frequently used to describe the combination of smoke and fog in California air. At the same time, the state government had to provide for its growing population. So the government built more schools and roads.

In the 1960s the United States passed civil rights laws to end the discrimination against African American citizens. But when things change, there are often problems. California, like most of the states, experienced violence during the civil rights movement. In 1965 there were riots in the Watts section of Los Angeles. More riots erupted in 1992 over a controversial trial of several policemen accused of beating an African American man.

Two politicians who began their careers in California later became President. Richard M. Nixon was elected in 1968 and 1972. He resigned the office in 1974 because of the Watergate scandal. Ronald Reagan was elected in 1980 and again in 1984.

A major earthquake again hit California in 1971. It was not as serious as the San Francisco earthquake of 1906, but 65 people in and around Los Angeles were killed. In 1989 another earthquake struck the San Francisco area, killing 63. And in 1991 and 1993, major fires burned thousands of acres including many homes. Another earthquake shook the Los Angeles area in 1994. This one killed at least 55 people and caused about $30 billion in damages.

Today, California's population and its economy are still growing. It is a worldwide center for technology, entertainment, and education. California is one of the most important agricultural, manufacturing, and mining areas in the country. Many thousands of people made their dreams come true in California. And the dreams are still coming true. It doesn't only happen in the movies.

Richard Nixon announced his retirement from politics after losing the 1962 California governor's election. He returned to politics in 1968 to run for President and won.

Ronald Reagan, the fortieth President of the United States, enjoyed a long career as a Hollywood actor before entering politics in 1966.

When the Earth Moves

Imagine what it would be like if the earth moved under your feet. Many Californians know the feeling all too well. That's because California's land structure is nearly perfect for earthquakes.

The San Andreas Fault is a huge break in the earth's crust, where the edges of two plates meet. The break is hundreds of miles long. It goes from southern California near the Mexican border to beyond San Francisco up the north coast of California. When this break, or fault, shifts even a little bit, the result is an earthquake.

In 1906 an earthquake struck San Francisco. The force of the quake broke electric and gas lines. This sparked fires all over the city. The quake had also damaged the city's water lines, so firefighters could not put out the flames quickly. Fires raged out of control for days. When the smoke finally cleared, most of the city was in ruins.

Another major earthquake hit the San Francisco area in 1989. This quake tore many major roads up out of the ground. Overhead roadways broke apart and fell down onto other roads below.

An earthquake hit Los Angeles at the other end of the San Andreas fault in 1994. Luckily, when the earthquake struck, it was 4:31 A.M. Most people

The Golden Gate Bridge spans 4,200 ft (1,280 m) at the entrance to San Francisco Bay, in the heart of the earthquake belt.

On April 18, 1906, San Francisco suffered a major earthquake; the resulting three-day fire destroyed the center of the city.

This photograph shows a section of freeway that crumbled following the 1994 earthquake.

were at home sleeping. Just hours later, the area's roads would have been jammed with cars carrying people to work. Thousands more might have been killed.

The 1994 Los Angeles earthquake could have ended in more deaths than the 1906 San Francisco quake. After all, there were many more people in Los Angeles in 1994 than in San Francisco in 1906. The Los Angeles quake killed at least 55 people. The 1906 San Francisco quake killed over 3,000 people. Why were so many more killed in the earlier earthquake?

One reason is that in recent years, construction methods have been improved. This helps protect California's buildings and water and gas lines against some of the force of earthquakes. Firefighting methods also have gotten better. Firefighters can now put out flames much more quickly. Rescue workers have better equipment and can act more quickly.

Earthquakes are scary. But scientists are working hard to find new and better ways to help Californians deal with them.

Cashing In on Resources— and Resourcefulness

California is rich. It's rich in natural resources. It's rich in people with ingenuity. It's rich in opportunity.

What does California have to boast about? To begin with, California is this country's leading farm state. And it has been since the middle of this century, when the state was only a hundred years old. California's agriculture is amazing. The rich soil was only waiting for proper irrigation. The state now produces more than half of all the fruits, vegetables, and nuts grown in the United States. Grapes are number one among these, but a short list of the others will also make your mouth water. There are almonds, apricots, walnuts, olives, dates, figs—the list goes on. The wine industry, made possible by the abundant grapes, produces ninety percent of all wine made in the United States.

About a third of California's farm income comes from livestock—beef and dairy cattle, poultry, sheep, and other animals. California's farm products include

Thousands of wind power machines, most of which have a capacity of 50–200 kilowatts, have been installed in the United States, particularly in California.

23

Here is an example of furrow irrigation in Kern County, California.

many varieties. You may be surprised to know that milk is its leading agricultural product.

But agriculture is not California's largest industry. The largest part of California's gross state product comes from what are called services. Ever since the first storekeeper sold the first pick to the first prospector, retail sales have been a huge part of California's economy.

California's tourism and recreation are big contributors to the service industry. In 1994 tourists and business travelers spent more than $54 billion in the state. Theme parks, such as Disneyland and Sea World, employ thousands and draw many thousands more as visitors. Recreation areas include national parks, such as Sequoia and Yosemite. Much of California's shoreline is accessible to the millions of tourists that visit each year.

Manufacturing also brings in more money for the state than farming does. Manufacturing produces the second largest part of California's income. Almost $134 billion worth of goods are produced in California every year. That includes transportation equipment such as aircraft, electronic components, communication equipment, printed materials, and many other products.

Mining is also a major part of California's economy. Gold, which is still mined, no longer leads the field as the state's most valuable mineral. That honor now goes to petroleum, but there is a lot of competition. California produces more different kinds of minerals than any other state.

But California has even more resources. California is the center of the motion picture industry. The film and television industry employs thousands of technically skilled workers. And the state's location on the coast makes it a primary distribution center between the United States and countries around the Pacific Ocean. In fact, it is the nation's largest center of imports and exports. California has a healthy commercial fishing industry, too. Ocean fish are the regular catch, including mackerel, squid, sardines, tuna, and sole. California has the

Disneyland was created by the film and television producer Walt Disney. The Anaheim amusement park attracts millions of tourists annually.

A technician installs a window in the cockpit of a commercial passenger airplane at a California assembly plant.

Yosemite National Park is one of California's natural treasures.

Cable cars such as the one pictured here are pulled by cables underneath the street. The first-ever cable car was installed in San Francisco in 1873.

seventh largest economy in the world. In fact, California's economy is greater than most countries today, including Canada and Russia. Taken on these terms, it is easy to say that California is indeed rich. Not the least of its riches are the people who plowed the new earth, built and rebuilt the towns and cities, and continue to forge their dreams into reality.

Giant redwoods grow in Redwood National Park in northwestern California. Redwoods, the world's tallest trees, often grow to more than 300 ft (90 m).

Southern California is famous for its beaches.

Imagination and the Silicon Valley

"I have to be many different people. I have to be a businessman sometimes and I'm pretty good at that, although it took some practice. And sometimes I'm a computer scientist and I talk to people in design and music and stuff about how computers fit into their worlds. And I'm all of those people, those are all real."

Those are the words of Jaron Lanier. He is a computer whiz whose imagination led him to develop a new idea about combining computers and music. Then he needed to sell his idea. California is the perfect place for Jaron Lanier.

An area around San Jose in Northern California has come to be called Silicon Valley. It is called that because so much work with computers is done there. Silicon is used in computer chips. Silicon Valley is one of the country's leading centers for developing computer hardware, software, and the networks that connect them.

Computer corporations and their factories settled in Silicon Valley in the 1960s and 1970s.

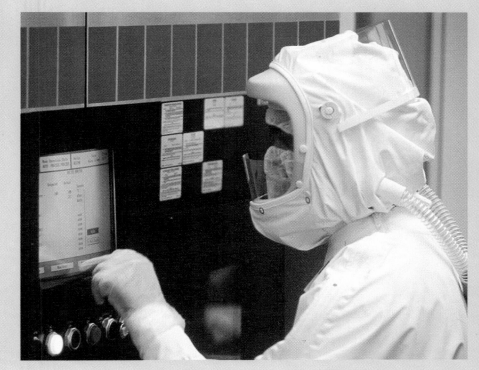

Computers once were used mainly by scientists. Now, advances in technologies have produced less expensive and more powerful computers that are used in many homes, offices, and schoolrooms.

In Silicon Valley there is a special combination of people who are experts not only in computers but also in making new businesses. Its main resource is the brainpower of the people who come from all over the world to try out their ideas.

Many new ideas that once seemed crazy have turned out to be the beginning of successful new businesses. Consider interactive television or multimedia programming. Silicon Valley welcomes creativity. Not only that, it tolerates failure more than most places seem to. How else can people find out what works?

Jaron Lanier belongs in Silicon Valley. He eagerly explained how musical instruments can be used with computers.

"These instruments speak to the human body and to the human heart and computers will eventually. They have to. Right now the worlds generated by computers live mostly on television screens. I think in the future it will be really quite different."

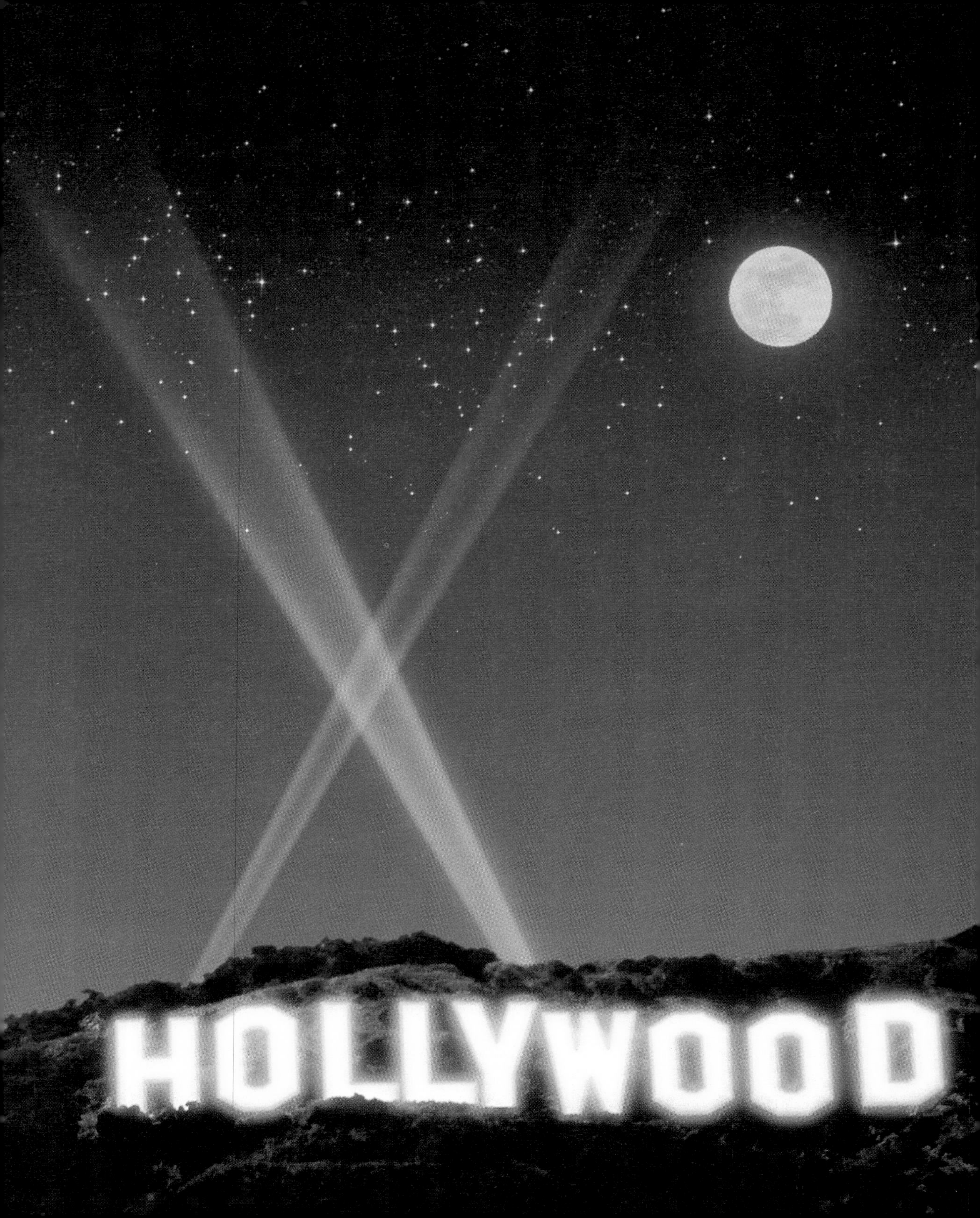
HOLLYWOOD

California, Here We Come

Americans have always gone west. From the days of colonial America, the direction of new frontiers was in the West. Some people would say that new frontiers are what California is all about. It's not that people in California come up with more strange, unusual, creative, and offbeat ideas than people in other parts of the country. It's that, wherever the ideas start, they seem to go west to California's new frontiers.

In California, you can live pretty much the way you want to so long as you don't hurt anybody else. You can wear clothes that might seem strange in other states. You can take classes in almost everything, from the martial arts to new forms of meditation to the latest in basket weaving.

You—and ten thousand others—can come to California to be a movie star. You can come to California and explore new art forms. You can come to California to start a new computer or software business. You and many, many others can come to

Hollywood has been at the heart of what attracts people to California.

California from another state or another country to start a new life. That's all part of California culture.

There's another part of California culture that goes back to the Native Americans, to the missions, to the early Spanish settlers, and to the Chinese immigrants. This other part is made up of Native American pottery, mission oak furniture, Spanish lace, and a grocery store in Chinatown. Add into it jade from China and silk from Japan. Sprinkle it with

above. San Francisco's Chinatown dazzles and sparkles at night.

below. Chinatown has one of the largest Chinese communities outside Asia.

gold dust, and season it with Paris fashions ordered by San Francisco society. This is the old California.

To see the new California, go down to the docks. This is where goods made in Asia come to America. Go to Silicon Valley where so much computer technology was born. Go to the factories, the canneries, the taverns. This is the world Nobel Prize winner John Steinbeck was born in and wrote about.

Yet, California is a mixture of old and new. Farming is still important — this is the biggest farm state in the country.

Writer John Steinbeck used California locales for many of his novels.

Steinbeck's *Cannery Row* is set among the fish canneries of Monterey.

The San Diego Zoo, founded in 1916, is noted for its exhibition of animals in open enclosures.

Spanish culture has deep roots in California. The dance company Ballet Folklorico del Pacifico help keep this culture alive.

Mexican culture can be seen in the new art and architecture.

People have been driving, sailing, flying, riding, and walking to California for hundreds of years. Immigrants continue to come to California. They all want to know what's going on in the land of something new.

Vineyards are abundant in the agriculturally rich San Joaquin Valley.

Murals by Paul Botello on stores and libraries in East Los Angeles usually contain a message.

Something Special

"On rainy days, I would just lie on my bed and I would think about probably being the first woman to go to the moon . . . I wanted to be something special, something where my parents could look back and say, 'Hey, that's our daughter and we're proud of her.'"

Cheryl Miller hasn't gone to the moon, but there is no denying that she is special. She is a young woman any parent could be proud of. She's a tall, strong, beautiful woman who was a basketball star and is now a coach.

Cheryl was the kind of basketball player on women's teams that Michael Jordan was on men's teams. She won an Olympic Gold Medal. She was an All-American four times. She was the only person to win the Naismith Award three times. That's the award in basketball that is like the Heisman Trophy in college football.

She played basketball for the University of Southern California, where she won every possible award and broke all records. In fact, she is the only basketball player in USC history, male or female, to have her jersey retired. She is considered the finest woman basketball player in history.

Cheryl Miller celebrates a victory during her playing days at the University of Southern California.

Miller seeks to become as successful in her coaching career as in her playing days.

Soon after graduating from USC, Cheryl received calls from women's professional basketball and volleyball leagues. She was also drafted by the United States Basketball League, which was a men's league.

Instead of turning pro, she stayed on at USC as an assistant coach. Later, she became a commentator for two television networks, commenting on both basketball and football.

Miller went on to become the head coach of women's basketball at USC and then head coach of the WNBA's Phoenix Mercury. What's the secret of her success? According to her, "America began as a dream, and without dreams, people can't reach their goals, because you have to look forward to something. You have to reach. You have to search for something. If you can see yourself doing it, if you can visualize yourself doing it, then you can achieve it. And in a dream, nothing goes wrong. And when you can put it in a reality and it goes right, then that's an accomplishment. But it all starts as a dream."

37

Hooray for Hollywood

You've probably heard of Hollywood, the place where many American movies are made. Hollywood has meant movies for as long as most people can remember. But in the early 1900s, most movies were made in New York City and New Jersey.

Movies quickly became big business. As they became more popular, people who made movies looked for ways to make their jobs easier. They wanted to shoot movies outdoors all year. This was hard to do in New York or New Jersey. Those places had too much bad weather.

Then the moviemakers discovered southern California. There the weather was perfect during most of the year.

A camera crew follows the action for this western movie.

These actors are getting ready to shoot the scene in which the cavalry saves the day.

Also, the California landscape offered a lot of variety. So movie people could shoot films about different parts of the world without leaving the state. They just used California's rich environment. There was the ocean. There was the desert. There were places that looked tropical, and there were snow-capped mountains. And none of these areas was too far from the district of Los Angeles known as Hollywood. It was there that the big movie studios were located.

The first movies were silent. Images moved on the screen, but there was no sound. Then in 1927 a movie called *The Jazz Singer* was produced. It was the first movie to use sound. Movie viewers were amazed. They called these movies "talkies." It was the beginning of a whole new way of making movies.

Some people didn't like the talkies. They wished that silent films had lasted. They said that talkies would lead to the end of movies. But that didn't happen.

Television first became popular in the 1950s. Many people thought it would replace the movies, but it didn't.

The Enterprise *is involved in an intergalactic shoot-'em-up.*

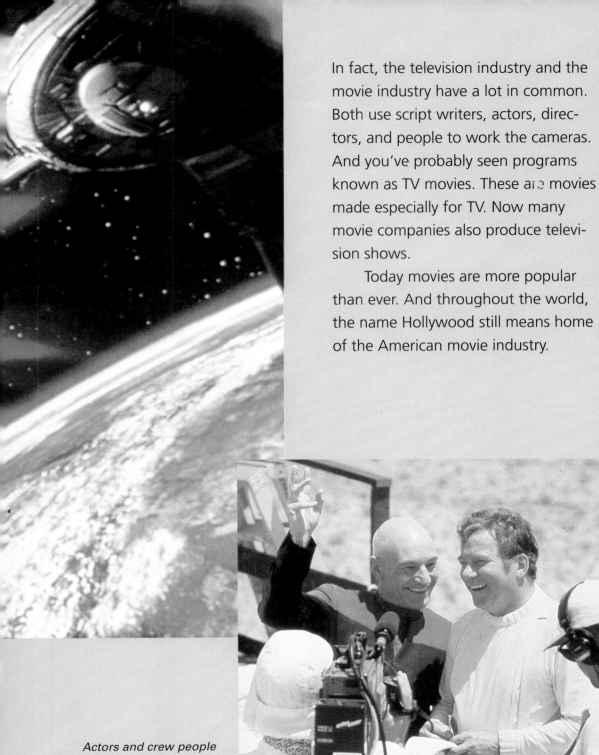

In fact, the television industry and the movie industry have a lot in common. Both use script writers, actors, directors, and people to work the cameras. And you've probably seen programs known as TV movies. These are movies made especially for TV. Now many movie companies also produce television shows.

Today movies are more popular than ever. And throughout the world, the name Hollywood still means home of the American movie industry.

Actors and crew people discuss the next scene.

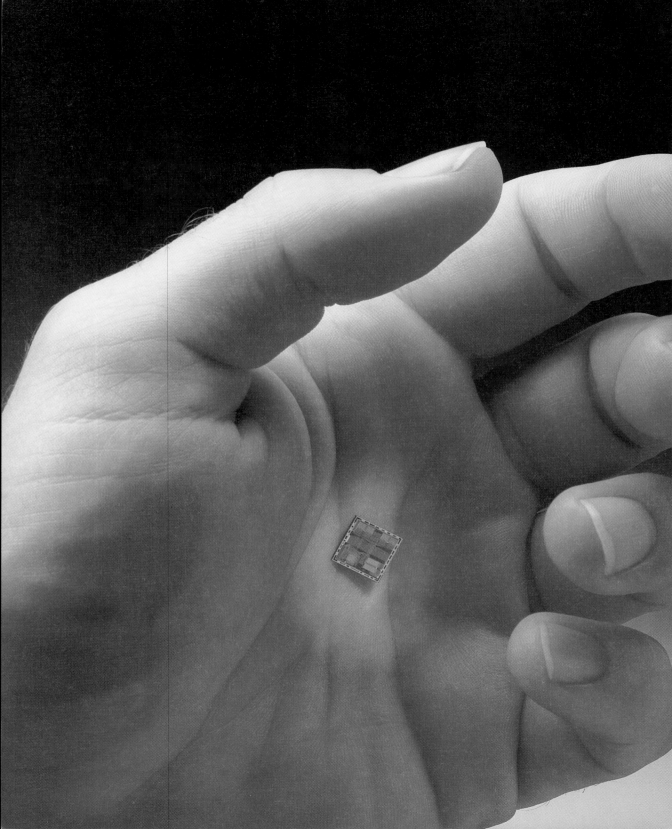

An Unofficial Leader

The state of California leads the rest of the United States in many ways. More people live there than in any other state. It produces more farm products than any other state. Its economy is larger than the economy of any other state. It includes the highest point in the continental United States—Mount Whitney. It also has the lowest point in the country—Death Valley.

California also leads the rest of the United States in other ways. Often we can get an idea of the way life may change in the rest of the country by seeing what is happening in California. One trend that has already started there is certain to be reflected in the rest of the country. The United States Census Bureau projects that by 2020 people of European descent will be a minority representing 34 percent of the population in California. Latinos will be 36 percent, Asians 20 percent, and African Americans 8 percent. In other words, every ethnic group will be a minority population.

Computer chips, such as this one, are essential for California's high-tech businesses.

There is also a trend toward more people moving in from other countries. California is perfectly located to be a bridge to the countries of Asia and the Pacific as well as to Mexico, Central America, and South America. California's economy will thrive even more as its new citizens work with their former countries to develop closer business connections.

This immigration trend will also cause some problems. For example, how can schools deal with so many students who speak so many different languages? But California will make the most of the situation. The new immigrants are another of California's many, many natural resources. After all, California is a place where people want to live. There is every reason to believe that California will continue to prosper because of them.

The variety of cultures in California will shape the future of this large state.

Important Historical Events

1540	The lower Colorado River is traveled by Hernando de Alarcón.
1542	Juan Rodríguez Cabrillo explores the coast of California.
1579	Sir Francis Drake sails into a body of water now called "Drake's Bay." He names the area New Albion.
1602	Sebastián Vizcaíno explores the coast and discovers the bay of Monterey.
1769	Spanish establish a mission at San Diego.
1812	Russians found Fort Ross.
1822	California becomes part of newly independent Mexico.
1846	The Bear Flag Revolt. War breaks out between Mexico and the United States over Texas.
1848	Treaty of Guadalupe Hidalgo at the end of the Mexican War gives both Texas and California to the United States. Gold is discovered at Sutter's Mill.
1850	California becomes the thirty-first state.
1864	During the Civil War, California remains in the Union.
1871	Rioting breaks out in Los Angeles when Chinese workers flood the job market.
1906	San Francisco is hit by an earthquake and fire.
1910	Hollywood is the movie capital of the world.
1930s	Homeless people pour into the state looking for work during the Depression.
1937	Golden Gate Bridge completed.
1942	After Pearl Harbor was attacked in 1941, Japanese Americans are forced into internment camps.
1965	Rioting breaks out in the Watts section of Los Angeles during racial tensions.
1968	Richard M. Nixon is elected president.
1971	A major earthquake hits California.
1974	President Nixon resigns because of Watergate Scandal.
1978	Proposition 13, which drastically reduces property tax revenue, is approved by voters in California.
1980, 1984	Ronald Reagan is elected president.
1989	An earthquake strikes the San Francisco area.
1991	Major fires burn thousands of acres and many homes in the Oakland-Berkeley area.
1993	Dozens of brush fires caused by six years of drought burn from Ventura County and around the Los Angeles Basin to the Mexican border.
1994	An earthquake shakes the Los Angeles area.

The "Bear Flag" was adopted as the official flag of the State of California in 1911. The white background symbolizes purity. The red in the star and in the bar stand for courage. The grizzly bear denotes great strength. The single star represents sovereignty.

California Almanac

Nickname. The Golden State

Capital. Sacramento

State Bird. California valley quail

State Flower. Golden poppy

State Tree. California redwood

State Motto. Eureka (I Have Found It)

State Song. "I Love You, California"

State Abbreviations. Calif. (traditional); CA (postal)

Statehood. Sept. 9, 1850, the 31st state

Government. Congress: U.S. senators, 2; U.S. representatives, 52. State Legislature: senators, 40; members of the assembly, 80. Counties: 58

Area. 158,648 sq mi (410,896 sq km), 3rd in size among the states

Distances. north/south 646 mi (1,040 km); east/west 560 mi (900 km); Coastline: 840 mi (1,352 km)

Elevation. Highest: Mount Whitney, 14,494 ft (4,418 m). Lowest: Death Valley, 282 ft below sea level (86 m. below sea level)

Population. 1990 Census: 29,839,250 (26% increase over 1980), 1st among the states. Density: 188 persons per sq mi (73 per sq km). Distribution: 93% urban, 7% rural. 1980 Census: 23,667,826

Economy. Agriculture: milk, beef cattle, greenhouse and nursery products, cotton, almonds, grapes, hay, tomatoes, citrus fruit. Fishing: tuna, salmon, shellfish. Manufacturing: transportation equipment, electrical equipment, food products, machinery. Mining: petroleum, natural gas

State Bird: California valley quail

State Flower: Golden poppy

Annual Events

★ Tournament of Roses Parade in Pasadena (New Year's Day)

★ Chinese New Year celebrations in San Francisco and Los Angeles (January or February)

★ Swallows return to San Juan Capistrano (March)

★ Fortuna Rodeo (July)

★ California State Fair in Sacramento (August/September)

★ Monterey Jazz Festival (September)

★ Hollywood Christmas Parade (November)

Places to Visit

★ Disneyland in Anaheim

★ Knott's Berry Farm in Buena Park

★ Missions throughout the state

★ Redwood Highway (US 101) from San Francisco to Oregon

★ San Diego Zoo

★ San Simeon (Hearst Castle) near San Luis Obispo

★ Scotty's Castle at Death Valley

State Seal

Index